Guided Meditation Scripts for Anxiety and Stress

Mindfulness meditation, breathing exercises, body scans, imagery and visualization for anxiety and stress relief, managing panic attacks, self-healing, chakra healing, deep sleep and relaxation.

By

Rayna Zara

Copyright © 2020 by Winnie Murugi

All Rights Reserved

No part of this book may be produced in any form by any electronic or mechanical means except in the case of quotation in articles or reviews, without written permission from the author.

Dedication

This book is dedicated to my son, Leo, for all the vibrancy and joy you bring into my life and for inspiring me to do better and be better at life.

Table of Contents

DEDICATION	3
INTRODUCTION	6
CHAPTER 1: QUICK GUIDED MEDITATION FOR ANXIETY	7
CHAPTER 2: GUIDED MEDITATION FOR ANXIETY	9
CHAPTER 3: GUIDED BODY SCAN MEDITATION FOR ANXIETY	15
CHAPTER 4: GUIDED MEDITATION TO MANAGE PANIC ATTACK	21
CHAPTER 5: GUIDED MEDITATION FOR SELF-HEALING	27
CHAPTER 6: GUIDED MEDITATION TO INSTANTLY RELIEF STRESS	35
CHAPTER 7: GUIDED MEDITATION FOR LETTING GO HURTS BY OTHER PEOPLE	37
CHAPTER 8: QUICK GUIDED MEDITATION TO GET CALM	44
CHAPTER 9: GUIDED MEDITATION TO COPE DURING DIFFICULT TIMES	47
SIT COMFORTABLY WITH YOUR LEGS CROSSED AND YOUR ARMS PLACED ON YOUR	47
CHAPTER 10: GUIDED IMAGERY FOR CENTERING AND GROUNDING	54
CHAPTER 11: GUIDED CHAKRA MEDITATION FOR ANXIETY AND STRESS RELIEF	59
CHAPTER 12: GUIDED MEDITATION FOR DEEP NIGHT SLEEP	69
CHAPTER 13: GUIDED MEDITATION TO STOP OVERTHINKING	80
CHAPTER 14: GUIDED MEDITATION FOR POSITIVE SELF-IMAGE	85
CHAPTER 16: GUIDED BREATHING MEDITATION FOR STRESS RELIEF	98
CHAPTER 17: GUIDED MINDFULNESS MEDITATION FOR ANXIETY	102
CHAPTER 18: GUIDED VISUALIZATION TO CALM AN OVERACTIVE MIND AND FOR RESTFUL SLEEP	107
CHAPTER 19: GUIDED MEDITATION TO INSTANTLY RELIEF ANXIETY	116
CHAPTER 20: GUIDED MEDITATION FOR CALM AND PEACE	120
CONCLUSION	126

Introduction

This book contains various meditation scripts for anxiety and stress. It contains guided visualizations and imagery, breathing exercises, body scans, and mindful exercises. The meditations range from 5 minutes up to 1 hour. It also incorporates quick relaxation techniques to help manage panic attacks or stress as well as long relaxation exercises for deep relaxation.

How to Use this book.

The Meditation scripts herein are ideal for use by yoga teachers, phycologists, counselors, meditation teachers, hypnotherapists or individuals. The Meditation scripts herein are ideal for use by yoga teachers, phycologists, counselors, meditation teachers, hypnotherapists or individuals. You can read them to your students/clients or record for personal or professional use but not for commercial use.

Each meditation has an indication for when you should be silent and for how long. Pace yourself as you read to ensure that your tone and pace give the audience a calming experience.

Chapter 1: Quick Guided Meditation for Anxiety

Sit comfortably in your chair and relax.

Gently close your eyes and begin to become aware of your breath. Bring your attention to your nose and notice the air as it comes in and goes out.

(20 seconds)

Take a deep breath in and release it slowly.

Take three more deep breaths.

(30 seconds)

Allow your body to relax and adapt to your breathing rhythm.

10 seconds

Notice the sounds in and out of the room; These sounds are not distractions but simply an expression of what is happening in your surroundings. Notice them and continue to breathe deeply and let your body continue to relax.

(30 seconds)

Is your mind wandering? It is okay for your mind to move from one thought to another. Slowly, focus your attention back to your breath. Notice how your chest is rising as you breathe in and gently falling as you breath out.

(20 seconds)

Make each inhale deep until your lungs cannot accommodate any more air.

(10 seconds)

And then breathe out completely allowing all the air out.

(10 seconds)

Keep focusing on your breathing, and if you feel your mind wandering gently guide it back to your breathing.

(30 seconds)

Breath in deeply.

Breath out gently.

Release all the expectations that you are holding on for this practice.

(10 seconds)

Your only responsibility at this moment is to consciously breath in and slowly release your breath.

Let go of all the judgments that you hold on this meditation. About whether you are being perfect or not.

(10 seconds)

As you breathe in notice your belly rise and as you breath out slowly notice the belly fall.

(20 seconds)

Allow yourself to relax and be present to this moment.

(30 seconds)

Now, take three deep breaths.

(30 seconds)

When you are ready, gently open your eyes and move your body slowly.

Chapter 2: Guided Meditation for Anxiety

Find a comfortable place to sit. Either on a chair or on the ground.

Adjust your posture accordingly and sit upright with your spine straight, neck tall and shoulders relaxed.

When you are ready, gently close your eyes.

Allow yourself to settle in the here and now.

(10 seconds)

Become aware of your surroundings. Notice any sounds around you. They may be loud or subtle. Maybe there is a sound of the clock ticking. Or, the humming noise of your air conditioning. Or, noise from the streets. Maybe you can hear the chirping of the birds outside. Or, it is completely silent. Just notice whatever sounds or silence in your environment.

(20 seconds)

Now, pay attention to your thoughts and notice what thoughts are popping up in your mind

(5 seconds)

What are you thinking about?

Are you thinking of your problems or your plans for the day?

Just become aware of the thoughts in your mind and let them go.

(10 seconds)

Now, bring your attention to your breathing.

Take a deep breath in through your nose and feel it fill your body.

(5 seconds)

Exhale completely and let the air leave your body.

(5 seconds)

Keep breathing deeply.

(30 seconds)

When you notice your mind wandering, just focus on your breathing and bring your attention back to my voice.

(30 seconds)

Feel the sensation in your nose as the air touches it.

(15 seconds)

Become aware of the air as it fills your lungs till they are fully inflated.

(5 seconds)

Then, gently release your breath and feel as your lungs become deflated. Feel the air leave your body through the nose.

(5 Seconds)

Now, return to your normal breathing rhythm. Let your breathing assume its own natural rhythm and just observe each inhale and exhale.

(30 seconds)

Remain alert and aware. If your mind wanders, bring your attention back to your breathing.

(30 seconds)

Now, notice the parts of your body that are in contact with the ground. Fell the support of the surface beneath you.

(10 seconds)

Direct your focus to your toes. Wiggle all your ten toes and feel them relaxing.

(10 seconds)

Make circles with your feet and let your ankles relax.

(10 seconds)

Notice your calf muscles and knees. Tighten the muscles around them and let go.

(10 seconds)

Bring your attention to your thighs, squeeze them together and release allowing them to relax.

(10 seconds)

Take your attention to your buttocks and feel them pressing down the surface beneath you. Relax them and let go of any tension around them.

(10 seconds)

Focus on your pelvic area and relax it.

(10 seconds)

Move your attention to your back. Do you feel any tension?

Tighten the muscles in your back and release them. Feel them relax as the tension around your back dissolves away.

(10 seconds)

Gently, take a deep breath through your nose and feel the air fill your entire body and then exhale completely releasing it.

(10 seconds)

Take a deep breath in and fill your belly completely allowing it to expand as much as possible and then exhale letting it fall and completely relax.

(10 seconds)

Round your shoulders and upper back and squeeze your chest muscles and then release and assume an upright position allowing the chest to open au.

(10 seconds)

Now, bring your attention to the shoulders. Squeeze them up towards your ears and then release them down letting go any tension as you feel them relax.

(10 seconds)

Stretch out your hands in front of you and make tight fists and then release spreading your fingers wide.

(10 seconds)

Rets your hands on your lap.

Drop your chin towards your collar bone and let the back of your neck stretch and release and tension.

(10 seconds)

Lift your chin as up as possible and allow the front of your neck to stretch and release tension.

(10 seconds)

Clench your jaw, close your eyes and tighten your facial muscles. Breath in deeply and hold your breath in for 7,6,5,4,3,2,1 and exhale gently as you allow your jaw and facial muscles to relax and then open your eyes.

(10 seconds)

Sit in the awareness of your entire body. It is relaxed and alert.

(30 seconds)

Bring back your attention to your breathing.

Inhale deeply and silently repeat the mantra 'I am inhaling.'

Exhale slowly as you silently say to yourself, 'I am exhaling.'

Keep breathing and reciting the mantras "I am inhaling", "I am exhaling".

(30 seconds)

When you notice your mind wandering, gently bring you attention back to your breathing and repeat the mantra.

I am inhaling.

I am exhaling

(30 seconds)

Gently direct your awareness to your body.

Feel the surface you are sitting on.

(5 seconds)

Notice the temperature on your skin.

(5 seconds)

Listen to the sounds around you.

(5 seconds)

Listen to your breathing.

(5 seconds)

Notice the sensations in your body.

(5 seconds)

Gently wiggle your fingers and your toes.

When you feel ready, open your eyes.

You are now ready to go on with your plans for the rest of the day.

Chapter 3: Guided Body Scan Meditation for Anxiety

Welcome to this body scan meditation. Think of the next 30 minutes as an opportunity to dwell in your body and to be in the present moment as it is.

(5 seconds)

Begin by finding a comfortable place to sit with your back straight but not stiff. If you are seated on a chair, allow your feet to rest on the ground. If you are seated on the ground, you may either cross your legs or straighten them. You could also do this meditation lying down with your feet extended in front of you and your hands resting beside your body. Adjust your body accordingly until you settle into a comfortable pose.

(10 seconds)

Gently close your eyes.

Become aware of the thoughts in your mind.

(10 seconds)

Our aim in this meditation is to release all the tension in your body and mind, so as to help you release stress and anxiety and to become calm and peaceful.

We will begin our scan from the top of our head to our toes. We will listen to our bodies and notice all the sensations then release all the tension and pains.

I will mention a part of your body; take your attention to that part of the body and scan it to detect any stress or tension around it. You will then visualize a yellow beam of energy shining on that part of the body as it washes away the pain, tightness or tension.

(5 seconds)

Now, bring your awareness to the top of your head and observe the sensations on this part of the body. Do you feel any tension? What sensations can you detect on this part of your body? Take a breath and send the energy light to it. See the light dissolve all the tension on the top of your head.

(20 seconds)

Bring your attention to your forehead. Is there tightness or any other noticeable sensation on this part of your body? Focus the yellow beam of energy to your forehead and let it melt away all the tension in this area.

(20 seconds)

Move your attention to your eyes. Scan them and check if they have any tension lodged in them. Do you feel any tightness behind your eyelids? Send the yellow beam of energy to the area around your eyes and feel as it dissolves the stress in your eyes.

(20 seconds)

Slowly move your awareness to your cheekbones and the cheeks. Observe whether there is any tension around them. Inhale and direct the yellow beam of energy on both cheeks allowing them to release tension and to relax.

(20 seconds)

Bring your awareness to your ears. Scan them for any tension and send the beam of energy to wash any tension that could be on your ears away.

(20 seconds)

Notice your mouth and jaw. Sense any tension around it. Shine the beam of energy on your mouth and jaw to clear away all that tension.

(20 seconds)

Become aware of your chin. Scan it for any tension. Now, shine the healing wave of energy to clear all the tension lodged in your chin. Feel as your chin relaxes.

(20 seconds)

Feel the back of your head. Slowly, scan it to detect any tension hidden in this area. Inhale deeply and let the yellow beam of energy consume all the tension held at the back of your head. As you exhale, allow your head to relax completely.

(20 seconds)

Take your awareness to your shoulders. Scan them for any tension. Now, send the energizing beam of energy to your shoulders and let it wash all the tension in that area.

(20 seconds)

Notice your chest. Notice how it rises and fall as you breathe in and out. Feel your heartbeat behind the chest. Scan every inch of your chest and check for tension lodged there. Focus the beam of energy to your chest. Let it clear all the tension, little by little until the entire chest area is fully relaxed.

(30 seconds)

Move your awareness to your back. Notice all the parts of your back from the upper back to the lower back, the spine and the entire torso. Scan the entire back for any tension, pain or tightness.

(5 seconds)

Shine the yellow beam of energy on your back. From the upper part of the back, to the middle part of the back and down to the lower back. Let this energizing light melt away any tension you are holding on to on your back.

(30 seconds)

Now, take your awareness to your stomach and the belly area. Visualize all the organs held within your rib cage and belly area. Your stomach, intestines, reproductive system, kidneys, liver, bladder, and all other organs. Scan your belly, ribcage and the organs beneath for tension or tightness.

(10 seconds)

Now, shine the beam of light to your stomach, rib cage and the organs beneath and let all the tension held on this area of the body dissolve.

(30 seconds)

Move your attention to your left arm.

Become aware of every part of your left arm; the biceps, triceps, forearm, palm and fingers.

(10 seconds)

Send the energy to your left arm to clear all the tension. Feel as the muscles in the whole of your left arm relax.

(10 seconds)

Now, move your awareness to your right arm. Notice all the parts of your right arm; biceps, triceps, forearm, palm and fingers. Scan for any tension in your arm.

(10 seconds)

Inhale and shine the beam of energy on your right arm and let all the tension in your right arm melt away. Feel as the right up relaxes.

(10 seconds)

Gently bring your awareness to your pelvis. Notice your buttocks, hips and groin area. Scan them for any tension, pain or tightness. Visualize the yellow beam of light shine upon your pelvis as it washes away all the tension leaving the buttocks, hips and groin completely relaxed.

(30 seconds)

Notice your left and right thighs. The thighs have the largest muscles in your body. As such, they can hold a lot of tightness and tension.

Bring your attention on the upper part of your right thigh and move your attention from the upper right thigh bit by bit up to the right knee as you scan for tension on the inner right thigh, top of the right thigh, back side of the right thigh and the outer edge of the right thigh. Now, visualize the relaxing beam of energy wash away tension from the upper part of the right thigh to knee.

(30 seconds)

Now, bring your attention on the upper part of your left thigh and move your attention from the upper left thigh bit by bit up to the left knee as you scan for tension on the inner left thigh, top of the left thigh, back side of the left thigh and the outer edge of the left thigh. Now, visualize the relaxing beam of energy wash away tension from the upper part of the left thigh to knee.

(30 seconds)

Become aware of the lower part of the legs. Notice your knees and the knee caps. Scan them for any tension and envision the yellow light dissolving all the tension that is on this part of your body.

(10 seconds)

Now, bring your attention to your left and right shins and calves.

(5 seconds)

Become aware of both of your ankles.

(5 seconds)

Scan your lower legs from the knees to your ankles for any pain or tension.

(10 seconds)

Inhale and shine the beam of energy beam on both of your legs from the knees to the ankles. As you exhale, feel your lower legs relax.

(15 seconds)

Gently move your awareness to your feet. Become aware of the bottom and the top part of your feet. Observe your feet and check for any tightness around them. Ease the tension there with the beam of light and feel as your feet relax.

(10 seconds)

Now envision the yellow beam of light shining on your entire body. It moves slowly from head to toes a sit washes away any remaining tension on your body.

(30 seconds)

It then moves from your toes to your head, bit by bit as it energizes every cell on your body.

(30 seconds)

Your body is now fully relaxed. You feel calm, peaceful, centered and grounded. Rest in this alert awareness of your body and in total relaxation for a moment.

(180 seconds)

Begin to deepen your breath. Gently wiggle your fingers and toes and when you are ready slowly open your eyes.

Namaste

Chapter 4: Guided Meditation to Manage Panic Attack

This guided meditation is ideal for when you are experiencing a panic attack.

Become aware of your physical position at the moment. It doesn't matter if you are sitting, standing or lying down. Just become aware of the place your body is.

If you want to make some changes for better comfort, you may stretch and then sit down comfortably.

(10 seconds)

Right now, you may feel as if your life is in danger and it is okay to feel this way. This is how your body and mind is responding to this moment here and now. It is neither right nor wrong.

I know that you are feeling scared because of the panic attack but it will pass.

Do you feel as if you cannot breathe properly?

(5 seconds)

You may be breathing in a good amount of air but not breathing out enough.

The good news is that we can fix it now.

Part your lips slightly and slowly push air from your system through your lips as if you are whistling. Pay attention to how the air whizzes out of your lungs completely.

Now, take a deliberate deep breath in. Can you feel how the air fills your lungs back without any effort?

(10 seconds)

Breathe out again through your mouth slowly pushing the air out.

(5 seconds)

Keep taking deep breaths.

(30 seconds)

Keep inhaling deeply and slowly push the breath out through your mouth.

(30 seconds)

Now, allow your body to adapt to its natural rhythm of breathing.

(30 seconds)

In case you feel like your breathing is becoming strained again, become more deliberate about ensuring that you are exhaling completely.

(30 seconds)

You are safe and in no danger at all. Panic attacks are horrible and may make you feel physically uncomfortable but that is all there is.

You are in no danger.

(10 seconds)

Now bring your attention to your body. Feel as your shoulders drop to their natural position and the muscles around them become relaxed.

(10 seconds)

Are you clenching your jaw? Loosen your jaw abit and allow it to relax. Let your tongue rest between your lower set of teeth. Parts your lips slightly so that they are not too tightly closed against each other.

(10 seconds)

Notice how your heartrate. It is beginning to slow down. Soon, it will resume its normal rate.

(10 seconds)

Notice your breathing is becoming deeper, calmer and quieter.

(10 seconds)

Allow yourself to relax.

(10 seconds)

Listen to the following affirmations. They will help your thoughts to calm down.

I know that I am safe.

(3 seconds)

I have the ability to overcome panic attacks.

(3 seconds)

I am aware that these panic attacks cannot harm me.

(3 seconds)

I am okay and safe even though my heart is racing.

(3 seconds)

I am calm.

(3 seconds)

I can envision what relaxation feels like.

(3 seconds)

I can envision my whole body feeling centered and relaxed.

(3 seconds)

I am safe and calm.

(3 seconds)

I know that I am safe.

(3 seconds)

I have the ability to overcome panic attacks.

(3 seconds)

I am aware that these panic attacks cannot harm me.

(3 seconds)

I am okay and safe even though my heart is racing.

(3 seconds)

I am calm.

(3 seconds)

I can envision what relaxation feels like.

(3 seconds)

I can envision my whole body feeling centered and relaxed.

(3 seconds)

I am safe and calm.

(10 seconds)

Now, begin to count backwards from 100, 99,98,96….

(30 seconds)

In this moment, here and now, you are safe. Allow yourself to get calm.

(30 seconds)

Now pay attention to your breathing. Do not adjust your breathing but notice as you breathe in and as you exhale.

(10 seconds)

Start to count each complete breath. A complete breath is made up of one inhale and a subsequent exhale.

(20 seconds)

Keep counting your breaths and when you lose count, simply start from the beginning.

(30 seconds)

Continue to notice and count each breath.

(90 seconds)

You are now calm and relaxed.

(5 seconds)

You are now calm and relaxed.

(5 seconds)

You are now calm and relaxed.

(5 seconds)

Let your body and mind continue to relax and calm down.

(60 seconds)

When you feel ready, you can open your eyes and familiarize with your surroundings.

Chapter 5: Guided Meditation for Self-Healing

Find a comfortable place to sit.

Rest your hands on your thighs with the palms facing up.

Settle into your pose and take a few deep breaths to ground and center you.

(60 seconds)

To heal your body, you need to become aware of the messages in the background in your subconscious mind.

Take a moment and ponder on the idea that your brain can process a lot of data in a second, but it can only be aware of a small amount.

(2 seconds)

Your body is performing divine functions all the time, every day.

(2 seconds)

While talking, sleeping, or driving; every second of every day, your brain is processing data to keep you functioning optimally.

(2 seconds)

You may not have considered this in the past, but it is time you consider and appreciate this temple that holds your thoughts, memories, your childhood beliefs and you as a whole.

(2 seconds)

Begin to breath in and breath out slowly.

(10 seconds)

Notice the sensations in your nostrils as you take a breath in and then release it.

(10 seconds)

How does it feel when the breath enters and exits your body?

(10 seconds)

Allow another deep breath and let it cleanse your system. Slowly breath out and release the tension from your body.

(10 seconds)

With each breath, allow your body to get heavy and relaxed.

Allow your body to relax from the sole of your feet to your head.

Notice your feet and allow them to relax. Do you sense any sensations on your feet?

(5 seconds)

Allow the relaxing sensation to move up your ankles, shins, calves and knees.

(5 seconds)

Let the sensation continue to move up your thighs and then to your hips, pelvis and the entire groin area.

(10 seconds)

Let the energy move your torso, from the belly to the rib cage and chest.

(10 seconds)

Then from your lower back, up the entire spine to the middle of the back and the upper back.

(10 seconds)

The relaxing energy moves down your shoulders, upper arms, elbows, lower arms, wrists, palms and fingers.

(10 seconds)

Let it go up to your collarbone, neck, face and head.

(10 seconds)

Feel it on your chin, lips, cheeks, and nose.

(10 seconds)

Become aware of your eyebrows and eyes. Notice the energy going through them.

(5 seconds)

Feel the relaxation spread to your forehead.

(10 seconds)

And then to your temples and ears.

(10 seconds)

And finally, to the top of the head and entire scalp.

(10 seconds)

Your entire body now feels calm and relaxed. You feel free and grounded.

(10 seconds)

Take a deep breath and hold it in. Let the energy of your breath fill all your muscles and then exhale gently through your mouth or nose and let you muscles relax even more.

(5 seconds)

Let your limbs become even more relaxed and heavy.

(5 seconds)

Take another breath in and let it relax your body further.

(5 seconds)

Release it and allow it to flow out with every little tension that could be remaining in your muscles.

(5 seconds)

Keep breathing slowly and smoothly.

(30 seconds)

Scan your body for any tension remaining. Do you notice any tension anywhere?

(10 seconds)

Take your relaxation energy into the still tensed parts of the body. Let it flow in that area and take the tension with it.

(10 seconds)

Think of the air you are breathing as a cleanser. Imagine that it can clear away all the tension in your body. Imagine that the air you breathe in has relaxation energy.

(5 seconds)

Visualize the tension being cleared out with every breath you take.

Relax- Can you feel how your body is relaxed and calm? Now enjoy that feeling for a few minutes.

(120 seconds)

Direct your attention to your body and think of the part that needs healing.

Envision your current state of being. Think of the physical illness that is troubling you.

It doesn't matter if it is a pain, an injury, illness or diagnosis. Whatever it is, think of it. Imagine this problem that you want its healing.

(5 seconds)

Picture your problem as darkness and the healing as a bright light. Envision the bright light flowing from your head to your toes.

(10 seconds)

Now, direct it to the darkness in your body and let it dissolve all the darkness in all the dark areas.

(30 seconds)

Your body has the ability to heal itself.

(5 seconds)

Notice the bright light improving your immune system, giving you strength, removing bacteria, toxins, and making a complete clean up of your system.

(20 seconds)

Envision the bright light flowing, touching and swirling over the darkness in the ailing part of the body.

(10 seconds)

Can you see the pieces of darkness being cleared from your system? Allow them to leave as you exhale.

(20 seconds)

Breathe in good health, tranquility, and healing — breath out stress, tension, ailments and all the problems in your system.

(20 seconds)

Let the bright light hover over the darkness as it performs its magic. Notice the darkness becoming smaller and lighter. The bright light is washing away everything that is harmful to your body.

(10 seconds)

Visualize your immune system boosting up; notice the cells going to their rightful places; performing their duties to heal your body.

(20 seconds)

Envision the bright light flowing through your body. Feel your body filled with relaxation feelings. Picture your ailing parts healing.

(20 seconds)

Let your body heal itself.

(10 seconds)

Witness your body feeling light like you have been unburdened.

(10 seconds)

Feel the extra space in your mind and your body.

(60 seconds)

You have reminded your body of its ability to heal.

(5 seconds)

You have approached the truth of your self-healing.

(5 seconds)

You have changed your course for good.

(5 seconds)

Embrace this change. Become aware that you are now your own healer.

(120 seconds)

Now it is time to get back to our normal level of wakefulness.

(5 seconds)

Feel your mind and body becoming aware of your body and its surroundings

(5 seconds)

Slowly deepen your breath as you direct your attention to your body.

(5 seconds)

Can you feel your heartbeat?

(5 seconds)

What sounds can you hear?

(5 seconds)

I will count to five. When I reach 5 gently open your eyes.

1

2

3

4

5

Welcome back.

Enjoy your renewed energy and a rejuvenated body. Have a lovely day ahead.

Namaste

Chapter 6: Guided Meditation to Instantly Relief Stress

Take a seat and when you are comfortable close your eyes.

(2 seconds)

Take a deep breath in and exhale gently.

(2 seconds)

Now direct your attention to your thoughts and envision yourself in a tranquil, focused and calm state.

(5 seconds)

Allow your mind to think of what you may feel is peaceful.

(5 seconds)

Think of what you may consider as tranquil.

(10 seconds)

Imagine what peace would sound like.

(10 seconds)

Think of how you may feel when you are calm and peaceful.

(10 seconds)

Maybe you are already focused, calm and peaceful.

(10 seconds)

If you are not, allow your unconscious mind to show you how to do it.

(30 seconds)

Are you feeling at peace and more focused?

(5 seconds)

Now, think of how you can incorporate that peace and calmness in your life.

(20 seconds)

Have you done that?

Good. I want you to understand that it is not difficult to create calm and peace in your life.

(10 seconds)

Take a deep breath and as you exhale, bring your attention back to the present moment.

(5 seconds)

Notice all the sounds around you.

(5 seconds)

You may open your eyes when you are ready.

Chapter 7: Guided Meditation for Letting Go Hurts by Other People

Lie down with your feet extended in front of you.

Let your arms relax by your side and the heels of your feet settle comfortably on the floor.

(2 seconds)

Gently close your eyes.

Allow your body to relax and get comfortable.

(5 seconds)

Now, bring your attention listen to any sound in the room. Identify the various sounds in the room.

(5 seconds)

Now bring your attention back to your body. Let it relax, feel it soften and allow it settle down.

(10 seconds)

Begin to take some deep breaths that effortlessly flow in and out of your body.

(60 seconds)

Now, allow your breathing to take its normal breathing rhythm. Let go trying to control it.

(60 seconds)

Feel the sensations as the air goes in to your nostril, dropping behind your throat and finally filling your lungs.

(10 seconds)

Then as it leaves your lungs, passes behind your throat and out through the nostril.

(10 seconds)

Observe how effortless and seamlessly the air enters and leaves your body.

(30 seconds)

If your mind begins to wander, observe that it is wandering and bring back your attention to your breathing.

 (10 seconds)

Continue to breath in and out without asserting any control.

(30 seconds)

Inhale and feel relaxation flow in your body. Exhale and release all the tension.

(10 seconds)

Breath in relaxation. Breathe out tension.

(10 seconds)

Become aware of your chest moving up and down with every cycle of breathing.

(20 seconds)

Notice how calm and relaxed your body is becoming.

(30 seconds)

Watch your breathing and be attentive to it.

If you notice that you are drifting off let my voice bring back your awareness to your breathing.

(30 seconds)

Breathe in relaxation. Breathe out tension.

(20 seconds)

Now, bring to mind the person that you want to let go. The person may still be in your life or not. They may have hurt you recently or in the past and you are no longer in contact with them.

(5 seconds)

Imagine him or her standing in front of you.

(5 seconds)

This person makes you feel negative emotions such as anger, resentment, bitterness and hurt, and you want to let go of the pain in your heart that they have caused you.

(5 seconds)

Direct your attention to your stomach and envision a silver cord that runs from your stomach to their stomach.

(10 seconds)

Feel it connecting the two of you.

Envision it pulsating as it gets energy from the connection.

(10 seconds)

Now, imagine that you are holding a pair of scissors in your hands.

(5 seconds)

Now take your hands towards the cord and notice as you cut through it. The cord may be tough and hard to cut but you gracefully keep cutting until you cut through.

(10 seconds)

Notice the cord break and separate.

(10 seconds)

Feel the connection between two of you dissolve. And, feel the freedom that accompanies your detachment.

(30 seconds)

Now, imagine a healing light surround the other person. Offer them your forgiveness, love, and blessings.

(10 seconds)

Watch as he or she slowly walks away from you.

(10 seconds)

You stomach now feels relaxed. The bitterness and resentment that was making it to become tensed is slowly dissolving.

(10 seconds)

You feel lighter, more peaceful and calm.

(10 seconds)

Now, pull the remaining energy cord to your stomach and seal it with a yellow light. Remind yourself that you have all your energy back with you and that you are safe.

(20 seconds)

Now scan your body for any signs of heaviness left behind.

(20 seconds)

Imagine yourself under a shower. Think of the water like a bright light and watch as it flows over your body. It is touching every part of your body from your head to your toes.

(20 seconds)

Let it cleanses your body of all the heaviness left behind.

(20 seconds)

Now, move your attention to your chest and imagine a green light in your heart center.

(5 seconds)

As you breathe in, the light expands and becomes bigger, as you breathe out the heart release all the tension. Keep breathing in and out gently as you allow the green light to dissolve all the tension and heaviness held in your heart.

(20 seconds)

Let the anger, bitterness and resentment go. Release all the anger and grief you feel. Let go of all the loss and self-loathing. Let whatever energy that is not serving you go. You deserve to be free of all the anger and resentment. You deserve to be at peace and to experience joy.

(30 seconds)

Continue to focus your attention to your heart. Allow the green light to become brighter and more vibrant.

(10 seconds)

Let the green light expand far above and around you forming an aura of protective and cleansing energy around you.

(10 seconds)

Now, bring to mind other people that may have hurt you either recently or a while back. Allow them a few inches into your aura of green energy. Look around and see each one of them. Remain Equanimeous and non-reactive as you look at each of them. Just become aware of their presence.

20 seconds

Now, repeat the following affirmations

I forgive you all that have hurt me.

(5 seconds)

I forgive myself for holding on to anger.

(5 seconds)

I let go all the anger, resentment, hurt and bitterness I feel.

(5 seconds)

I invite love and kindness into my life.

(5 seconds)

The aura of green light continues to expand around you as the people who hurt you walk away.

(10 seconds)

Now, visualize yourself living a peaceful and harmonious life. How do you feel? What does your everyday look like? How is your interaction with other people?

(20 seconds)

Let the green light return to your heart center. Remember it is always available for you whenever you need.

(5 seconds)

Become aware of your breathing. Notice your breath as it moves from your nostrils to your lungs.

Notice the air as it leaves your body and finds its way back to your immediate surrounding.

(20 seconds)

Continue to remain aware of your breath.

(120 seconds)

Gently wiggle your fingers and your toes. Move your head from side to side.

(10 seconds)

Become aware of the room you are in and the sounds in it.

(10 seconds)

When you are ready, open your eyes. Stretch your body a little bit and feel the new energy and bring it to the rest of your day.

Chapter 8: Quick Guided Meditation to Get Calm

Find a comfortable place to sit either on a chair or on the ground. Adjust your posture accordingly until you find a relaxing and alert pose with your spine tall and shoulders relaxed.

(10 seconds)

Allow yourself to rest in your seated posture and to become present to this moment.

(10 seconds)

Remember that your past is gone and your future has not yet arrived. The present moment is what is real.

(5 seconds)

Therefore, let go the need to dwell in the past or he future and presence yourself to the now.

(5 seconds)

Notice what happening in your body in this moment. How is your breathing? Is it shallow or deep, is it rapid or slow? Become aware of each breath.

(10 seconds)

Continue paying attention to your breath.

(20 seconds)

Follow your breath from the point you start breathing.

Feel your stomach expanding.

(10 seconds)

Notice how it rises and falls with every breath that you take.

(20 seconds)

Become aware of how your breath slows down at every end.

Follow it from the beginning till it starts to slow down and then starts again.

(30 seconds)

Embrace your breath with all your attention and care.

Hold it like a mother would hold her baby.

(10 seconds)

Do not drop the breath.

(5 seconds)

Let your thoughts reside in the background.

Enjoy the rise and fall of your abdomen.

(1 minute)

Notice how your mind keeps producing thoughts but do not follow them.

(5 seconds)

Just maintain your focus on your breathing.

(10 seconds)

Feel at ease and enjoy the comfort in the present moment.

(20 seconds)

Take a deep breath and release slowly.

(10 seconds)

With every breath, release all the tension in your mind and body.

(10 seconds)

With each breath, relax your face and smile.

(10 seconds)

Do you feel any sensation in your body?

(5 seconds)

Become aware of the air going through your breathing system and back.

(10 seconds)

Notice the sounds in your surroundings but do not respond to them.

(5 seconds)

Continue breathing peacefully and don't get lost in your thoughts.

(20 seconds)

Smile and feel contented.

Do you notice how your mind is calm and peaceful?

Feel rested and free.

Namaste

Chapter 9: Guided Meditation to Cope During Difficult Times

Sit comfortably with your legs crossed and your arms placed on your thighs palms facing up

(5 seconds)

Take three deep breaths and exhale completely with each breath.

(30 seconds)

Keep breathing deeply allowing your body to become relaxed.

(60 seconds)

Now, bring your attention to the challenges you are facing. Without thinking too much about them, just identify them one by one.

(20 seconds)

How are you feeling? Are you mad, sad, stressed, in pain, or sorrowful? Identify the emotions that stand out for you in this moment.

(10 seconds)

Realize that these emotions are a manifestation of the chemical process taking place in your body. Therefore, notice them without judgement or getting involved in them.

(15 seconds)

Do not try to push them away either. Instead become a curious observer. Notice how intense they are. Are they manifesting on a specific part of the body? For instance, can your feel a heaviness at your solar plexus, or do your shoulders feel tight? Or is your heart feeling a bit faster. Have you lost your smile and your jaw is tightly clenched and lips tightly closed? Become aware of the parts of the body that these emotions are manifesting.

(30 seconds)

Whatever feelings you are experiencing, you do not need to be ashamed of them just because you perceive them as negative feelings. Be open to them. See them as a way of your body responding to various circumstances and happenings. It is alright, you are human, and you are allowed to feel how you are felling in this moment.

(60 seconds)

Now, begin to deepen your breaths.

(20 seconds)

Take notice of your hands and tighten them into fists.

(5 seconds)

Make the fists tighter and notice tension build up in your hands.

(5 seconds)

Release the tight grip on your fists and allow your entire hand to become limp.

(5 seconds)

Become aware of your shoulders.

(5 seconds)

Think of how they would feel if they were relaxed. Now, tighten the muscles around the shoulders and then relax them.

(20 seconds)

Take your attention to your face.

(5 seconds)

Narrow your focus to your jaw. Tense your entire jaw. Now allow the jaw to relax and notice as the tension melt away.

(5 seconds)

Now scan your whole body and search for hidden stress in the muscles. Relax every area that you can senses tension.

(120 seconds)

Scan one more time to see if there is any part of the body that is still tensed even if just a little bit. Tighten the body part and allow it to relax.

(60 seconds)

Now scan the whole body from your head to your toes. Take a deep breath in and tightly squeeze all the parts of your body. Hold your breath in and continue to squeeze your muscles some more. Begin to exhale slowly as you relax the entire body.

Become aware of how your body is feeling now.

You are gaining control of your negative emotions.

You are no longer hiding these emotions.

You have taken a step to allow yourself to feel them but not giving them control over your life.

Remember that allowing yourself to acknowledge these negative feelings is an act of courage.

(10 seconds)

Once again, begin to take deep breaths.

(20 seconds)

With the expansion of every inhale, allow your body to create room in your heart for positive emotions. With the contraction of every exhale become aware of your ability to cope with difficult times and emotions.

(5 seconds)

Keep breathing in and out as you allow your body to create more space for grace, strength and courage.

(60 seconds)

Now, allow your breathing to adapt to its normal rhythm and just observe it.

(60 seconds)

Think of a time, you were delighted and at peace. When was it. How was life then. How did you feel? Remember that moment in details.

(20 seconds)

Allow yourself to relive that moment and for the emotions you felt then to fill your body and mind.

(20 seconds)

Let the memory and emotions of that time remind you that no matter all the negative emotions of fear, distress, doubt, hatred, overwhelm, and mistrust you are feeling right now, you will overcome and experience joy and peace again.

(10 seconds)

Think of a person, place, or experience related that brings you joy. Visualize it or the person in details and let the joy of thinking about it or them fill your heart.

(20 seconds)

Think about what is most important in your life. Maybe it is your family, career, friends, or relationship?

Despite these difficult times, you still have something to be grateful for. Identify what is going well in these areas of your life and express gratitude for it. Let it encourage you that all is not lost, that you will overcome.

(60 seconds)

Take a deep breath and hold it in. Allow your heart and mind to fill with gratitude. Exhale gently as you continue to express gratitude for even the smallest things that you take for granted like your heart beating or your ability to talk among others.

While things are difficult at this moment, you can still choose to make the most out of life. Be deliberate about thinking empowering thoughts that sooth you, support you and encourage you. Choose to be compassionate and kind to yourself. And manage your time and energy in a way that allow you to cope the best way possible.

(20 seconds)

Visualize yourself getting to the other side of whatever difficulty you are experiencing. How does it feel to have surmounted this challenge or obstacle? You will be stronger and wiser on the other end. And for that reason, you choose not to give up on yourself or to allow yourself get drained by all the negative emotions you are feeling.

(20 seconds)

Make a promise to yourself to be kind to yourself and be grateful even though for just one thing amid the challenge you are facing.

(10 seconds)

As we wind up this meditation, repeat the following affirmations:

1. I feel the fear, the doubt and the difficulty but I choose to show up everyday
2. I have what it takes to overcome these challenges
3. Even though I am faced with a difficult situation, I completely love and accept myself
4. I offer myself compassion, love and kindness during these tough times
5. I allow myself to feel the pain but not allow it to maim my spirit and my being.
6. This too shall pass
7. Better days are coming
8. I choose to hang in there with optimism
9. Every day I deliberately incorporate activities in my life that sooth my soul
10. I let go all the anger, pain and resentment I feel
11. I invite peace, calm and mental stillness into my life

12. My inner guidance and the infinite intelligence of the universe is guiding me towards finding solutions and coping with my challenges

13. Everyday things are getting better

14. I trust the process of life to work out things for my highest good.

15. All the information I need to resolve this challenge comes to me easily.

16. I am surrounded by people who offer me the support I need

17. I allow myself to learn the lessons from this situation

18. I am courageous and brave

19. I am grounded and supported

20. All well is my life

Understand that difficult moments will pass. They may seem like they are fixed in your life at the moment, but with time, they shall pass. Nothing is permanent and this too shall pass. So, hang in there. Muster the courage and strength you need. You will overcome.

(20 seconds)

Chapter 10: Guided Imagery for Centering And Grounding

You may practice this meditation in a seated position either on a chair or the ground.

Begin by finding your comfortable seated position. Adjust your body as need be until you are comfortable and alert.

(10 seconds)

Sense the support the chair, cushion or ground offers to the parts of the body that they are in contact with.

Feeling that support, allow your pelvis and buttocks to ground down and your upper body to elongate in an alert and upright posture.

Your shoulders are directly stack over your hips and dropping downwards.

Rest your hands on your lap or knees.

Release the weight of the arms to gravity.

Gently close your eyes and begin to be aware of your entire body.

Your feet… legs…thighs…pelvis…lower back… upper back…shoulders…abdomen…ribs…chest…. arms… neck and head. Just being aware of yourself as a physical being.

(20 seconds)

Now bring your awareness to your breath, and the actual physical sensations that manifest when you breath. Feel each breath as it comes in and goes out…

(20 seconds)

Allow the breath to be just as it is, without trying to change or regulate it in any way.

(20 seconds)

Allow it to flow easily and naturally, in its own rhythm and pace, knowing you are breathing perfectly well right now.

(30 seconds)

Allow the body to be still and as you sit here feel a sense of dignity, a sense of resolve, a sense of being complete, whole, in this very moment, with your posture reflecting this sense of wholeness.

(45 seconds)

As you sit here in still calmness, bring to mind a magnificent mountain that you have either seen or one that you imagine.

Gradually allow your imagination of this mountain to come to focus.

Have an overall sense of the mountain's shape, high and low peaks, its base, it steep and gently sloping slopes as well as the large base of bedrock that the mountain is rooted in.

Notice how beautiful, unmoving and majestic the mountain is.

What other aspects of the mountain can you see? Maybe the highest peak is disappearing into the low hanging clouds, or there are streams and waterfalls cascading down the slopes of the mountain, some rocks are protruding on the slopes or a part of the mountain is covered with trees.

(30 seconds)

Now embody the qualities of the mountain. See yourself as a majestic, unmovable and still mountain. Just like the bedrock grounds the mountain, you are held firmly by the ground beneath your feet or bottoms.

(10 seconds)

Grounded in the sitting posture, your head becomes the lofty peak, supported by the rest of the body and affording a panoramic view.

Your shoulders and arms the sides of the mountain. Your bottoms and legs the solid base, rooted to your cushion or your chair. Experience in your body a sense of uplift from deep within your pelvis and spine.

(10 seconds)

With each breath, as you continue sitting, becoming a little more a breathing mountain, alive and vital, yet unwavering in your inner stillness, completely what you are, beyond words and thought, a centered, grounded, unmoving presence.

(10 seconds)

As you sit here, becoming aware of the fact that as the sun travels across the sky, the light and shadows and colors are changing virtually moment by moment in the mountain's stillness, and the surface teams up with life and activity… streams, melting snow, waterfalls, plants and wildlife.

(10 seconds)

As the mountain sits, seeing and feeling how night follows day and day follows night. The bright warming sun, followed by the cool night sky studded with stars, and the gradual dawning of a new day.

(10 seconds)

Through it all, the mountain just sits, experiencing change in each moment, constantly changing, yet always just being itself.

It remains still as the seasons flow into one another and as the weather changes moment by moment and day by day, calmness abiding all change.

(10 seconds)

In summer, there is no snow on the mountain except perhaps for the very peaks or in crags shielded from direct sunlight. In the fall, the mountain may wear a coat of brilliant fire colors. In winter, a blanket of snow and ice.

(10 seconds)

In any season, it may find itself at times enshrouded in clouds or fog or pelted by freezing rain. People may come to see the mountain and comment on how beautiful it is or how it's not a good day to see the mountain, that it's too cloudy or rainy or foggy or dark.

None of these matter to the mountain, which remains at all times its essential self. Clouds may come and clouds may go, tourists may like it or not. The mountain's magnificence and beauty are not changed one bit by whether people see it or not, seen or unseen, in sun or clouds, broiling or frigid, day or night. It just sits, being itself.

(10 seconds)

At times visited by violent storms, buffeted by snow and rain and winds of unthinkable magnitude. Through it all, the mountain sits. Spring comes, trees leaf out, flowers bloom in the high meadows and slopes, birds sing in the trees once again.

(10 seconds)

Streams overflow with the waters of melting snow. Through it all, the mountain continues to sit, unmoved by the weather, by what happens on its surface, by the world of appearances… remaining its essential self, through the seasons, the changing weather, the activity ebbing and flowing on its surface.

(10 seconds)

In the same way, as you sit in meditation, you learn to experience the mountain, you embody the same central, unwavering stillness and groundedness in the face of everything that changes in your life, over seconds, over hours, over years.

You experience constantly the changing nature of mind and body and of the outer world, you have periods of light and darkness, activity and inactivity, moments of color and moments of darkness. You experience storms of varying intensity and violence in the outer world, mind and body and through it all you remain deeply rooted and grounded.

(10 seconds)

By embodying the mountain, you can emulate its strength and stability as your own. You can personify its energy to support you so that you encounter each moment with mindfulness, equanimity and clarity.

You will begin to understand and know that your thoughts, feelings, perceptions, emotional crises and everything else that happen is like the ever-changing weather and you are like the magnificent mountain. Ultimately you will come to know a deep stillness and wisdom.

(60 seconds)

May you know your strength, may you find equanimity and may you be grounded and centered.

(60 seconds)

Begin to gently deepen your breath. Wiggle your fingers and your toes. When you are ready gently open your eyes.

15 seconds fade out

Chapter 11: Guided Chakra Meditation for Anxiety and Stress Relief

Find a comfortable position either seated or lying down and gently close your eyes.

(5 seconds)

Become aware of your surroundings. Are there any sounds in your immediate environment?

(5 seconds)

Is it warm or cold? Is the air humid?

(5 seconds)

The air you are breathing is it warm or cold? Does it have a smell or it is odorless?

(5 seconds)

Now, become aware of the parts of your body that are in contact with the ground. Allow your body to become limp and for the surface beneath you to support you.

(10 seconds)

Notice any sensations on your skin.

(10 seconds)

Notice any sensations on the different parts of your body.

(10 seconds)

Begin to take deep breaths.

(20 seconds)

Let the inhales and exhales allow you relax.

(20 seconds)

Notice as your chest rise and fall with every inhale and exhale.

(10 seconds)

Feel the sensation in your nostrils as you breathe in and out.

(10 seconds)

Become aware of the difference in temperature of the air that you are inhaling and the one that you are exhaling.

(20 seconds)

Now bring your attention to your tailbone, the bottom of your spine where the root chakra is located. Visualize a red circle of energy pulsating on the area around your tailbone. Take some deep breaths and visualize the energy going to your root chakra, easing any tension held on this part of your body

(30 seconds)

This root chakra is responsible for connecting you to the energy of the earth. When your root chakra is balanced, you feel grounded and supported. (On the other hand, when your root chakra is overactive, you feel jittery and anxious. It might also manifest physically as digestive problems, lower back pain, hip pain, ovarian issues and prostate issues in men.)

(To balance your root chakra every day, incorporate grounding activities such as meditating and prayer in your everyday life. Also spend time in nature.)

(10 seconds) *Say to yourself*

Repeat the following mantras to help you get grounded:

"I am here."

(5 seconds)

"I deserve to be here."

(5 seconds)

"The Earth is my support."

(5 seconds)

Take a few deep breaths here as you pay attention to the surface beneath you.

(30 seconds)

Now bring your attention to the area just below the belly button where your sacral chakra is located. Visualize an orange circle of energy pulsating around this area. Take some deep breaths and visualize the energy going to your sacral chakra, easing any tension held on this part of your body

(30 seconds)

This sacral chakra is responsible for your creative and sexual energy. When your sacral chakra is balanced, you feel motivated and relish in the joys of life without needing to over indulge. You are also sexually and creatively expressive. (On the other hand, when your sacral chakra is overactive you have addictive and overindulgent tendencies. When it is underactive you experience a lack of passion, decreased sex drive and lack of creativity. Physically, an manifest as depression, obesity, hormonal imbalance and addiction.

To balance your sacral chakra, engage in creative activities often. Repeat the following mantras, Say to yourself.

"I am infinitely creative"

(5 seconds)

"It is ok for me to enjoy life"

(5 seconds)

"I let go the need to overindulge"

Take a few deep breaths as you pay attention to your sacral chakra.

(30 seconds)

Bring your attention the area on the top of your stomach where your ribs meet. This is where your solar plexus chakra is located. Visualize a yellow circle of energy pulsating around this area. Take some deep breaths and visualize the energy going to your solar plexus, easing any tension held on this part of your body

(30 seconds)

This solar plexus chakra is responsible for your sense of confidence and personal power. When your solar plexus chakra is balanced, you feel confident, a sense of wisdom, as sense of personal power and you are decisive. Otherwise, when it is underactive, you may feel timid, indecisive, insecure and needy. When it is overactive you may feel too energized, greedy, angry and have a need to control and micromanage.

Physically, in imbalanced solar plexus chakra manifests as digestive issues or issues on internal organs such as kidneys, liver, appendix and pancreas.

To balance your solar plexus chakra, recite self-esteem and self-confidence affirmations.

Repeat the following affirmation: *Say to yourself*

"I am enough"

(5 seconds)

"I am worthy"

(5 seconds)

"I am confident"

(5 seconds)

Take a few deep breaths here as you pay attention to the area around your solar plexus.

(30 seconds)

Now, move your attention to center of your chest where your heart chakra is located. Visualize a green circle of energy pulsating around this area. Take some deep breaths and visualize the energy pulsating in your chest area, easing any tension held on this part of your body

(30 seconds)

The heart chakra is responsible for your ability to give and receive love. It is also associated with compassion, kindness, empathy, joy and peace. of confidence and personal power. When your heart chakra is balanced you give and receive love with ease. You are kind and compassionate to others. When it is overactive, you may find it difficult to set healthy boundaries for yourself or you may experience interpersonal relationship issues. When it is underactive, you might find it difficult getting close to other people.

To balance your heart chakra, offer yourself self-love. Treat yourself with compassion and kindness and extend the same to other people. Engage in acts of service that are within your boundaries.

Repeat the following affirmation: *Say to yourself*

"I accept myself"

(5 seconds)

"I am willing to learn to love myself unconditionally"

(5 seconds)

"I am kind and compassionate to myself and others"

(5 seconds)

Take a few deep breaths here as you pay attention to the area around your heart center.

(30 seconds)

Now, move your attention to your throat where the throat chakra is located. Visualize a purple circle of energy pulsating around this area. Take some deep breaths and visualize the energy pulsating in your throat area, easing any tension held on this part of your body

(30 seconds)

The throat chakra is responsible for expressing your personal truth with clarity, love and kindness. If your throat chakra is overactive or interrupting others. (When it is underactive, you may feel shy or opt to remain silent even on issues that are important to you. Physically, an imbalanced throat chakra may manifest as loss of voice, throat pain, cavities, or mouth ulcers)

When speaking always think:

"Is it the truth?"

"Is it necessary?"

"Is it kind?"

To balance your throat chakra practice expressing your emotions and truths.

Repeat the following affirmation:

"It is ok for me to speak my truth"

(5 seconds)

"Even when I feel like my truth does not matter, I will say it anyway"

(5 seconds)

"It is becoming easier and easier for me to speak my truth"

(5 seconds)

Take a few deep breaths here as you pay attention to the area around your collarbone and throat area.

(30 seconds)

Now, move your attention to the space between your eyebrows. This is where the third eye chakra is located. Visualize an indigo circle of energy pulsating around this area. Take some deep breaths and visualize the energy pulsating on the area around you're the space between your eyebrows, easing any tension held on this part of your body

(30 seconds)

The third eye chakra is responsible for intuition. It is believed to give the brain access to information that is beyond the material world and what your five senses can detect. When it is balanced you feel in tune with both yourself as well as the physical and material world. You will receive intuitive messages with ease.

When it is overactive you may become obsessed with getting psychic information. On the other hand, when it is underactive, you may feel spiritually disconnected. Physically, an imbalanced third eye chakra may manifest as headaches, vision problems or sinuses.

To balance your third eye chakra, spend time in nature and engage in spiritual activities regularly.

Repeat the following affirmation:

"I am tuned in to my intuition"

(5 seconds)

"I am in alignment with the universe"

(5 seconds)

"I am divinely guided"

(5 seconds)

Take a few deep breaths here as you pay attention to the area between your eyebrows.

(30 seconds)

Now, move your attention to the top of your head where your crown chakra is located. Visualize a white circle of energy pulsating around this area. Take some deep breaths and visualize the energy pulsating on the area on the top your head, easing any tension held on this part of your body.

(30 seconds)

The crown chakra is responsible for pure conscious energy. It is the center of enlightenment and spiritual connection with your higher self. When it is balanced you feel in tune with your higher self and divine consciousness.

(When it is underactive, you may feel spiritually disconnected. Physically, an imbalanced third eye chakra may manifest as headaches.)

To balance your crown chakra, engage in spiritual activities regularly and balance the other chakras.

Repeat the following affirmation:

"I am spiritual being experiencing humanness"

(5 seconds)

"I am connected to my highest self"

(5 seconds)

Take a few deep breaths here as you pay attention to the area around the crown of your head.

(30 seconds)

Once more visualize the various energy circles pulsating on all your chakras. A red circle of energy on your tailbone, orange circle of energy two inches below your belly button, a yellow circle of energy on your solar plexus, a green circle of energy on your chest, a purple circle of energy on your throat, an indigo circle of energy between your eyebrows and a white circle of energy on the crown of your head. See all the circles of energy vibrating simultaneously.

(30 seconds)

Now, bring your attention your body. Notice how your body feels and any sensations. Notice how calm, grounded and peaceful you feel and rest in this awareness.

(60 seconds)

Begin to deepen your breath.

(10 seconds)

Gently move your head from side to side.

(10 seconds)

Come to stillness and when you are ready gently open your eyes.

Chapter 12: Guided Meditation for Deep Night Sleep

This meditation is best done as the last activity of the day to help you relax into deep sleep. Before you begin, do whatever you need to and settle down in your bed. Lie down with your legs stretched out to front and hands resting beside your body. It is best not to wear earphones with this one as you may fall asleep in the middle.

Settle down into your pose and let's begin.

Make a mental scan of the whole of your body and notice how you feel emotionally and physically.

(10 seconds)

Check for any pain or tension in your body. Check for any tiredness.

(10 seconds)

move your attention from one part of the body to the next from head to toes.

(60 seconds)

During this meditation for deep night sleep, we will concentrate on quieting the mind and releasing the tension in your body. This will help to calm your mind and you will drift into restful sleep.

Now, take a deep breath and hold it in for a few seconds.

(6 seconds)

Slowly exhale the air, and allow all the tension in your body to leave.

(6 seconds)

Become aware of your thoughts.

(5 seconds)

What are you thinking about?

Are you thinking of your plans for the next day or your day's activities?

Are you feeling worried about someone or something, perhaps?

Just notice your thoughts as they arise and go away then new ones arise and go away.

(60 seconds)

For a moment allow your mind the freedom to think.

Let it roam freely and accept all the thoughts that come to it.

(30 seconds)

Let your mind be free to worry about all the challenges in your life.

(10 seconds)

Think of the people you love.

(10 seconds)

Think of your career, job, calling or business.

(10 seconds)

Think of your relationships.

(10 seconds)

Do you have a pet, perhaps? Think about it.

(10 seconds)

Think of the long-overdue plans and goals that you have not accomplished yet.

(10 seconds)

Do not limit your mind.

Let it roam freely.

(60 seconds)

All those thoughts are legit, but for now we will let them be and not dwell on them.

It is time to allow your mental chatter to quieten or slow down so that you can have a relaxing sleep.

Resting sufficiently will energize your body and mind to enable you carry on tomorrow's roles and duties properly.

(5 seconds)

Now, become aware of how your body feels at this present moment.

(10 seconds)

Do you feel tired and tense in any part of your body?

Notice the parts that feel tired.

(30 seconds)

Direct your attention to those parts one by one.

Take a deep breath, and as you exhale, visualize all the tension leaving each part.

(30 seconds)

Continue to breath deeply, and with every exhale, visualize all the tension leaving the tensed part of the body.

(30 seconds)

Become aware of how a sense of relaxation and ease in your body.

Allow the feeling of relaxation to grow throughout your body.

(10 seconds)

With each breath you take, visualize as the feeling of relaxation spreads across your body.

(20 seconds)

Now, bring your attention to your right heel where it makes contact with the ground.

Don't move it; use your imagination.

Send awareness to the right foot big toe.

(5 seconds)

Now send your awareness to the second toe, third, fourth, and pinkie.

(5 seconds)

Become aware of the whole right foot.

Let go any tension you may be holding to on the left foot.

(5 seconds)

Now bring your awareness to the calf on your right leg.

(5 seconds)

Notice the ankles and bring your awareness upwards to the shin.

(5 seconds)

Let the awareness flow to your right knee and feel it softening and relaxing.

(5 seconds)

Now, bring your awareness to your right thigh.

Feel the front of the thigh, the back, and the thigh bone. Hold the entire right thigh in awareness.

(10 seconds)

Take your awareness to your right buttock.

Let it become heavy and then relaxed.

(5 seconds)

Now move your awareness to your left buttock. Let it become heavy and then relaxed.

(5 seconds)

Become aware of the left thigh. Notice the top, bottom, and the entire bone of your left thigh. Allow it to let go any tension and to relax.

(10 seconds)

Drop your attention downwards to your left knee. Imagine the knee cap softening.

(10 seconds)

Bring your awareness to the left shin all the way down to the ankles.

(5 seconds)

Notice the left calf and let it relax.

(5 seconds)

Scan the entire left leg from the thigh to the ankle.

(10 seconds)

Bring your awareness to the left heel. Allow it to be heavy. Feel the sole of your left foot and let go any tension

(10 seconds)

74

Become aware of the big toe on your left foot.

(5 seconds)

Move your awareness to the second toe, third, fourth, and the pinkie.

(5 seconds)

Let the whole foot relax.

(5 seconds)

Notice both legs from the buttocks, thighs, knees, calves, shins, ankles, feet to the toes lying heavy and relaxed on the surface beneath you. Allow both legs to relax completely.

(20 seconds)

Now, become aware of your belly. Do you know how your stomach unravels when you are hungry?

Now, imagine it unravelling and relaxing.

Visualize your entire belly area, the muscles and organs becoming relaxed.

(15 seconds)

Now move your attention to your chest. From the ribs up to the collarbones.

Visualize your entire chest area, the muscles and organs becoming relaxed.

(15 seconds)

Bring your attention to your lower back. Now, move it up from the lower back to the bottom of your neck allowing the entire back to relax.

(5 seconds)

Notice both shoulders and allow them to completely relax.

(5 seconds)

Bring your awareness to your right-hand bicep, then the tricep and allow your upper arm to relax.

(5 seconds)

Become aware of your elbow and let it relax.

(5 seconds)

Let the right forearm relax.

(5 seconds)

Now, bring your awareness to the right wrist and let it relax.

(5 seconds)

Slowly move your awareness to the palm of the right hand and the back of your right hand.

(5 seconds)

Bring your attention to your right thumb, then the second finger, to the middle finger, ring finger and the pinkie.

(5 seconds)

Become aware of the entire right hand and let it relax.

(5 seconds)

Now, take your awareness to the left bicep and tricep and let it relax.

(5 seconds)

Become aware of your elbow and let it relax.

(5 seconds)

Let the left forearm relax.

(5 seconds)

Now, bring your awareness to the left wrist and let it relax.

(5 seconds)

Slowly move your awareness to the palm of the left hand and the back of your left hand.

(5 seconds)

Bring your attention to your left thumb, then the second finger, to the middle finger, ring finger and the pinkie.

(5 seconds)

Become aware of the entire left hand and let it relax.

(5 seconds)

Feel your whole body on the left side.

Allow it to get heavy and relaxed.

(10 seconds)

Feel your whole body on the right side.

Allow it to get heavy and relaxed.

(10 seconds)

Bring your attention to your neck. Imagine that your neck is lengthening and releasing any tension.

(5 seconds)

notice your entire scalp and it relax.

(5 seconds)

Bring your attention to your face. The forehead, cheeks, ears, jaw, chin, lips and nose. Allow the entire face to relax.

(5 seconds)

Take your attention to your right eye and then the left eye. Notice if you have tightly shut the eyelids and allow them to relax.

(5 seconds)

Notice how your body feels now. Is it relaxed? Are there parts that are still tensed?

(5 seconds)

Send relaxing energy to the tensed parts.

(20 seconds)

Calmly say, "I am relaxed" three times.

(20 seconds)

Now, concentrate on counting.

Start at number one and count up to ten. Allow your body to relax even more with each number that passes.

Let us count together, slowly paying attention to each number and your body.

1

Feel your body become more relaxed.

(5 seconds)

2

Notice the peace and calm that surrounds it.

(5 seconds)

3

Feel all the tension leaving, and in its place comes relaxation.

(5 seconds)

Visualize number 4 and notice how your legs and arms are relaxed and heavy.

(5 seconds)

5- Feel a deep wave of relaxation washing over you.

(5 seconds)

6- Your body is deeply relaxed and peaceful.

(5 seconds)

7- Your mind is free from all baggage.

(5 seconds)

8- Relaxed and heavy

(5 seconds)

9- Let your mind float and relax.

(5 seconds)

10- You have reached a level of deep relaxation.

(5 seconds)

Now begin to count backwards from 10 to one.

(2 seconds)

Begin from 10 and slowly count nine and continue on your own.

(60 seconds)

You are now peaceful

-comfortable

(2 seconds)

-warm

(2 seconds)

-relaxed

(2 seconds)

-heavy

(2 seconds)

Accept this feeling

(2 seconds)

Nurturing

(2 seconds)

Confident

(2 seconds)

Quiet

(2 seconds)

Smooth

(2 seconds)

You are at peace with yourself

(2 seconds)

You are now fully relaxed, and you can now drift off to deep sleep.

Drift off to sleep- deep and restful sleep.

Goodnight.

Chapter 13: Guided Meditation to Stop Overthinking

Find a comfortable place and assume an alert posture either seated or lying down.

(5 seconds)

Once you are comfortable and settled in, gently close your eyes.

(5 seconds)

Bring your awareness to your breath.

Notice how your chest falls and rises with every breath.

(10 seconds)

Notice how your lower stomach falls and rises as well.

(10 seconds)

Feel as your ribs expand with every breath you take. Feel as they, contract with every exhale you release.

(10 seconds)

Become aware of your breathing rhythm. Is it fast or slow? Is it deep or shallow?

(30 seconds)

Become aware of every inhale and every exhale.

(20 seconds)

Notice the temperature in your skin. Is there a dominant sensation of warmth or coolness?

(10 seconds)

You could be warm in some parts of your body and cool in others.

It is okay; none is right or wrong.

(10 seconds)

Notice how warm or cold your fingers are.

(10 seconds)

Notice how warm your toes and feet are.

(10 seconds)

Become aware of any sensation in your legs and arms.

(20 seconds)

Acknowledge that they may change any time. Understand that these sensations are not permanent.

(10 seconds)

Become aware of your body parts that feel relaxed.

(20 seconds)

Now, notice the other parts that may feel tensed, tired or even sore.

(20 seconds)

Just allow your mind to observe and take note of every sensation in your body.

(30 seconds)

Notice how your body functions are automated. The body knows what to do and how to do it. Did you know that in every second your body is carrying out billions of biochemical processes? Without your control or guidance.

(10 seconds)

In this moment here, you are in the right place.

You do not need to be somewhere else.

This is your moment to get calm and grounded.

It is a great time to be in this present moment.

(60 seconds)

Now, begin to slow you breathing. Make your inhales and exhales longer.

 (20 seconds)

Continue to breathe deeply. Long inhales and long exhales.

(20 seconds)

Notice the power of your mind. That is your awareness of how your body responds naturally to your thoughts.

All you are doing is allowing your mind to think in its ordinary and natural way.

(20 seconds)

Your mind just asked your body to reduce its pace to calmer breathing.

Without any effort, your body obeyed, and your breathing slowed down.

(10 seconds)

Notice how you become relaxed with every new breath.

(10 seconds)

Now, allow your breath to assume its natural rhythm and take note of every breath.

(20 seconds)

Take note of any thought that may pop in your mind.

(10 seconds)

Become aware of any judgment within you.

(10 seconds)

Check if your mind wants you to create any evaluations.

(10 seconds)

Simply relax and take note of what thoughts your mind is instructing you to create.

Observe; be keen on your mind.

It is okay if you find nothing.

Sometimes you may find distractions or boredom.

(60 seconds)

Now, slowly divert your attention to your breathing.

Breathe in deeply.

(5 seconds)

Breathe out gently.

(5 seconds)

Become aware of your surroundings.

(5 seconds)

what sounds do you notice in your immediate environment?

(5 seconds)

Listen for the distant noises.

(5 seconds)

Then bring your attention back to the space you are in and notice any sounds whether subtle or loud.

(5 seconds)

Now bring your attention to your body. Begin by moving your fingers and toes.

(5 seconds)

Make circles with your head and the come back to stillness.

Take a deep breath and when you are ready slowly open your eyes.

(5 seconds)

Chapter 14: Guided Meditation for Positive Self-Image

Find a quiet place where you can sit or lie down comfortably.

(5 seconds)

Take three deep breaths and exhale completely.

(30 seconds)

Keep breathing deeply.

(30 seconds)

Now notice your hands – your fingers, the space between your fingers, nails and palms.

(10 seconds)

Notice your feet – your toes, the space between your toes, toe nails and the entire feet.

(10 seconds)

Visualize a relaxing light flowing from your head to your toes that washes away any tension and leaves you feeling relaxed.

(30 seconds)

Now, think about your perspective of yourself. How would you feel if had great self-esteem, confidence and self-acceptance?

(30 seconds)

A positive self-image is not perfection.

It is okay to have areas that need improvement.

It is alright to have things that you may want to change in yourself.

(10 seconds)

A positive or negative image is portrayed in self-talk.

When you make positive remarks about yourself, you maintain healthy self-esteem.

Contrary, if you make negative comments, you damage your self-esteem.

(10 seconds)

Positive thinking is portrayed in how you treat yourself.

Sometimes people change to be unique.

Sometimes they also change to be similar to others to avoid standing out.

There is nothing wrong with being different.

There is also nothing wrong with being similar to others.

(20 seconds)

Now, envision yourself having a jar of pure liquid relaxation. The liquid is in your favorite color.

(5 seconds)

Envision yourself having a soft paintbrush as well.

(5 seconds)

Visualize yourself opening the jar and dipping the brush in it.

When I mention a body part, envision yourself painting it slowly and notice as that part becomes relaxed.

Face

(5 seconds)

Neck and throat

(5 seconds)

Shoulders

(5 seconds)

Lower and upper back

(5 seconds)

Your right hand

(5 seconds)

Your left hand

(5 seconds)

Chest and stomach

(5 seconds)

Bottoms and hips

(5 seconds)

Your left thigh then the right thigh

(5 seconds)

Your left knee then the right knee

(5 seconds)

Right calf and left calf Calves

(5 seconds)

Left and right shin

(5 seconds)

Right foot ankles and left foot ankles

(5 seconds)

Left foot and right foot

(5 seconds)

Toes- all the ten toes

(5 seconds)

Notice how your body becomes relaxed from head to toes.

(5 seconds)

Become aware of any parts of the body that may need extra relaxation paint.

(5 seconds)

Pass some extra strokes of the relaxation paint on those parts.

(30 seconds)

Notice how much calmer your mind is.

(10 seconds)

Now, envision yourself with a positive self-image.

Imagine yourself as successful.

Imagine yourself as confident.

Imagine yourself as likable.

(20 seconds)

If you held yourself in high esteem, how would you show up in your everyday life.

(30 seconds)

What would you do differently?

(30 seconds)

Mistakes are a reminder that you are human. When you make mistakes, purpose to learn from them, and grow every day.

Offer yourself kindness and compassion when handling your mistakes, flaws and imperfections.

(20 seconds)

Let confidence, joy, and happiness grow inside you.

(20 seconds)

Now, I will count backward from three, and when I reach one, gently open your eyes.

Three

Two

One

Chapter 15: Guided Meditation for Total Body and Mind Relaxation

Find a quiet place and assume a comfortable and alert posture.

(5 seconds)

bring your attention to your breathing. Take a deep breath in through your nose and observe as your stomach expands.

Hold it for a few seconds and exhale slowly through your mouth.

Once again breath in through your nose, hold your breath in and then breath out through your mouth.

Continue to breathe deeply, in and out through your nose.

(20 seconds)

Observe the movement of your stomach when you inhale and exhale. Notice how it expands and then contracts.

(20 seconds)

With each inhale allow your body to be washed with cleansing energy and with every exhale allow tension to leave your body.

(20 seconds)

Breath in as you say "I am relaxed", as you breath out say "I let go tension and stress".

(30 seconds

Breathe in

Breathe out

(30 seconds)

Now, bring your awareness to your feet.

Breathe in deeply fill your feet with cleansing energy, exhale slowly let your feet relax.

(10 seconds)

Notice tension ease off from your feet..

Notice your toes relaxing.

(10 seconds)

Now, move your attention to your legs.

Envision a white light surrounding your legs and getting rid of all the tension there.

All the stiffness held in your shin evaporates in the air.

All the tension held in your calves diffuses in the air.

(10 seconds)

your legs feel heavy and relaxed.

(10 seconds)

Now, let your breath assume its normal rhythm.

(15 seconds)

Breathe in and envision a bright light moving to your upper legs.

Breathe out. Notice as it clears away all the tension.

Your thighs are now relaxed.

(20 seconds)

Become aware of your hips.

Breathe in

Envision a bright light surrounding your hips and bottom.

Visualize the bright light relaxing all the muscles in your hips and bottom.

As you breath out, visualize the light carrying away all the tightness and tension from your hips and bottom.

(20 seconds)

Take another deep breath.

Notice a bright light filling your spine.

Notice as your spine becomes bright and energetic.

As you exhale, visualize as the bright light release all the tension between the discs and the joints in your spine.

(20 seconds)

Notice how relaxed your body is becoming.

(20 seconds)

Take your awareness to your stomach.

Take a deep breath and observe as your stomach expands.

Breathe out slowly and observe the air carrying all the tension from your stomach.

(20 seconds)

Breathe in a beam of light.

Notice as it travels to your heart and chest.

Notice the light circling your heart in slow motion.

Become aware of your heart chakra opening.

Can you see the beautiful flower radiating a green light?

Feel all the tension in that area disappear, and your heart and chest relax as you exhale.

(30 seconds)

Take your awareness to your throat.

Take a deep breath.

Notice as the light enter through your nose to your throat.

Notice it getting rid of all the tension in your throat as you exhale.

(20 seconds)

Take a deep breath and release it slowly.

Become aware of your neck.

Notice all the tension lodged in your neck muscles.

Envision your neck moving in a circular motion.

Send the bright light to your neck and instruct it to clear all the tension in that area.

Breathe out all the stress and tension in your neck.

(20 seconds)

Breath in a beam of light.

Become aware of your face.

Notice all the tension in your eyes, nose, forehead, and jaw.

Notice as the light relaxes all your facial features.

Feel as your face become completely relaxed as you exhale.

(20 seconds)

Envision a green healing light on top of your head.

Notice as it circles your crown chakra.

Notice as the energy travels down to your body.

Feel it covering your entire head.

(10 seconds)

Notice it dropping through the veins in your neck.

Feel it dropping further to your shoulders.

(10 seconds)

Observe as the green light fills your left and right hand.

As it drops down to your body, it becomes stronger.

Notice as it fills your heart.

Notice how relaxed your chest is

(20 seconds)

Your heart expands with love and compassion.

(10 seconds)

Notice the green light dropping to your stomach and unraveling any tension left there.

It also flows down your entire back.

Feel it traveling between the veins and the muscles in your back.

Feel the green light strengthening your spine.

(20 seconds)

Now, notice as it circles your hips and bottom.

Feel it tightening and releasing the muscles in your bottom and hips.

Notice as it relaxes your hips and bottom.

(10 seconds)

Visualize the green light separating to form two streams.

Observe as each stream of green light takes its natural course on the left and right thigh.

Feel the two streams relaxing the muscles in your left thigh and right thigh.

Feel the muscles relax.

(10 seconds)

Notice as the two streams drop further to your knees.

Feel it behind the knee caps.

Feel it carry the tension away from your knees.

Notice how your knee caps are feeling relaxed.

Feel all the muscles and veins in your knees relaxing.

(10 seconds)

Become aware of the two streams of green light drop to the lower parts of your legs.

Feel them relaxing the muscles in your calves.

Notice all the tension in your calves disappearing.

The green light flows into your shins easing any tension here.

Your lower limbs now feel relaxed and at ease.

(30 seconds)

Become aware of your ankles.

Scan for any tension or pain in your ankles.

Allow the two streams of green light to drop simultaneously to your ankles.

Notice your ankles relaxing.

Notice the green light-absorbing all the tension in your ankles.

(10 seconds)

The two streams of green light then flow into your feet taking away any tension.

(10 seconds)

Once again, envision the beam of green light flowing seamless through your body from the top of your head to your toes.

Notice as it rushes down to your body, filling it with the green light.

Feel as this light touches all your parts that need healing.

Think of any weakness in your body.

Think of the parts that are hurting.

Think of any part that has an injury.

Become aware of the green light touching those parts and healing them completely.

(30 seconds)

Your entire body is now flooded with this green light.

Feel it expanding your aura.

Feel it releasing energy that your aura requires.

Become aware of the glow in your aura, chakras, and your entire body.

Visualize your aura becoming complete with no imbalances or holes.

(30 seconds)

Feel as your body relaxes even more.

(10 seconds)

Your mind is calm and clear.

(10 seconds)

Rest in this calmness and centeredness for a while.

(90 seconds)

Take your awareness to your surroundings and your body.

Listen to your gentle breathing.

(5 seconds)

Listen to the sounds in the room.

(5 seconds)

Listen to the sounds far away.

(5 seconds)

Wiggle your fingers and toes.

(5 seconds)

Shake your head from left to right.

(5 seconds)

Move your shoulders up and down.

(5 seconds)

Gently open your eyes.

Welcome back to consciousness.

You are now ready to face the day with a relaxed mind and body.

Enjoy the rest of your day.

Chapter 16: Guided Breathing Meditation for Stress Relief

Begin this practice by sitting down comfortably and closing your eyes.

Take four deep breaths through your nose, taking in the air entirely and releasing it fully through your nose and mouth.

(20 seconds)

Gently, let your breath adapt to its normal breathing rhythm.

(5 seconds)

Pay attention to every inhale and exhale.

(5 seconds)

Feel the air entering your nostrils and moving down to your lungs.

Notice how your chest and belly expand.

(10 seconds)

As you exhale, become aware of the air leaving your lungs through the nostrils.

Notice how your chest and belly contract.

(10 seconds)

Observe any difference between the air you inhale and the air you exhale.

Is the air you inhale cooler than the air you exhale?

(10 seconds)

Listen to any sounds in your immediate environment.

You are alert and aware that these are sounds not distractions. Hear them just as they are.

(10 seconds)

Maybe, there is no sound in your immediate environment. Notice the silence.

(10 seconds)

Now, bring your attention to your breathing in its natural rhythm.

(10 seconds)

Be observant of it without being judgmental. Notice as it comes in through your nose and then goes out after a few seconds.

(20 seconds)

The rhythm is effortless and seamless.

(20 seconds)

If you notice your mind wandering, observe the thoughts as they pop in your mind.

Let each thought go as if it was a feather being carried by the wind.

(10 seconds)

Place every thought that pops on a leaf and observe as the wind sweeps it.

(5 seconds)

Now, bring back your awareness to your breathing.

Your breath helps you to return to the practice when your mind wanders.

When you observe your mind wandering, just notice the thought and let go.

(20 seconds)

Learn to divert your focus back to your breath when distracted.

(20 seconds)

Notice as your stomach rises when you breathe in and as it falls when you breathe out.

(10 seconds)

When you get distracted by any pain or discomfort in your body, just breathe.

When you notice that you are getting distracted by any feelings, be it happiness, frustrations, or sadness, just breathe.

All you have to do is to notice when your mind wanders.

Let the thoughts pass without judging them or pushing them away.

(10 seconds)

Do not cling to the thought either.

Do not wish it were a different thought.

Observe it and redirect your mind to focus on your breathing.

(30 seconds)

Take a deep breath in.

Exhale slowly.

(5 seconds)

Keep breathing mindfully in and out.

(60 seconds)

Observe the air as it gets into your system and follows it back as its exit.

Mindfully be in this present moment as you breathe in and out.

(90 seconds)

As we wind up our practice, expand your attention to your body.

Notice any sensations in your body.

(20 seconds)

Expand your awareness to your immediate environment. Notice any sounds or silence, the temperatures and the general energy of the space you are in.

(20 seconds)

When you are ready, you may open your eyes.

Namaste

Chapter 17: Guided Mindfulness Meditation for Anxiety

Sit down comfortably on a chair or the floor.

(5 seconds)

With your spine lengthened, bring your attention to your breathing.

Conscious deep breathing is a great tool for managing anxiety.

Begin to take deep breathes through your nose and then breath out through your nose.

(30 seconds)

Keep your mouth closed on the exhale and continue to take deep breaths.

(30 seconds)

Make you inhales deep and your exhales even deeper.

(60 seconds)

Now, hold your breath for a count of 5 between the inhale and exhale, and between the exhale and the next inhale.

(60 seconds)

With each inhale completely fill up your lungs and with exhale completely empty out your lungs.

(60 seconds)

Each inhale fills up your lungs with oxygen supplying the body with the cleansing energy to help you cope when feeling anxious. With each exhale, the body releases pent up energy and creates room for calm, peace and being grounded.

(20 seconds)

breath in calm breath out anxiety.

Inhale "I am calm", exhale "I am surrendered"

(20 seconds)

Make yourself comfortable, and do not try to fight the anxiety. When gross sensations of anxiety come up, graceful deepen your breaths and observe the sensations and feeling of anxiety. Without resisting it, become curious, study it, observe it.

(20 seconds)

Fighting it only strengthens it.

Accept this feeling of anxiety. It is a feeling and it will pass sooner or later.

(20 seconds)

Repeat the following after me.

I am feeling anxious, but it is okay.

(5 seconds)

It will pass, and I will be safe.

(5 seconds)

I may be frightened, but I know that I am in no harm.

(5 seconds)

I am relaxing comfortably as I wait for this feeling to pass.

(5 seconds)

I have the power within me to relax and calm myself until it passes.

(5 seconds)

I am feeling anxious, but it is okay.

(5 seconds)

It will pass, and I will be safe.

(5 seconds)

I may be frightened, but I know that I am in no harm.

(5 seconds)

I am relaxing comfortably as I wait for this feeling to pass.

(5 seconds)

I have the power within me to relax and calm myself until it passes.

(5 seconds)

Breathe in slowly.

Exhale slowly.

Continue to think calming and comforting thoughts.

(20 seconds)

When you are anxious, your body prepares to either fight or run away.

This makes your heart pump more oxygen to your muscles to give them the strength to either fight or escape.

When you have an anxiety feeling and in no danger, the adrenaline being produced is not being used.

You are trembling or feel overwhelmed because your body is ready for action.

(10 seconds)

You can reduce the trembling by shaking off the tension from your body.

Shake your hands as if you want to dry them.

Let them become limp as you shake them vigorously.

(5 seconds)

Visualize drops of water dropping from your fingertips.

Imagine those drops are tension.

Visualize as the tension is shaken from your body.

Stop shaking your hands and notice how you feel. Maybe you feel a bit at ease or maybe the anxiety is still there. Just observe.

(10 seconds)

Keep breathing deeply as you allow your mind to become calmer.

As you breathe in, tell yourself that you are getting calm.

Breathe out and remind yourself that you are getting relaxed.

Breathe in calm

Breathe out tension

Breathe in relaxation

Breathe out anxiety

(20 seconds)

Now, let us focus on relieving stress from our muscles.

Become aware of your muscles.

Notice the ones that may feel tired or tight.

(5 seconds)

If you are clenching your teeth, lower your jaw and let it relax.

(5 seconds)

Drop your shoulders.

Notice how they became loose and relaxed.

(5 seconds)

Move your arms in a circular motion.

Raise your arms up and actually stretch.

(10 seconds)

Slowly, release all the muscles and let your hands rest on your laps.

Straighten your spine and let your body adapt an upright posture.

You are now relaxed and rode off anxiety. You can practice this meditation any time you feel anxious.

Move your head from left to right.

Look side by side and then straight ahead.

(10 seconds)

And the come back to the center.

When you are ready, gently come open your eyes.

Chapter 18: Guided Visualization to Calm an Overactive Mind and for Restful Sleep

Lie down on a bed and adjust your body to a comfortable posture where you can safely fall asleep.

As your body and mind relax, you may fall asleep.

If you don't, it is still alright as your body and mind will be relaxed as well.

Begin to breath in deeply.

Exhale gently.

(5 seconds)

Inhale and exhale slow and calm breaths and allow your body to relax.

(20 seconds)

You don't have to do anything; just take slow and deep breaths.

(20 seconds)

Take a deep breath in and slowly release it, prolonging the exhale.

(10 seconds)

Take another breath in and then exhale slowly.

(10 seconds)

Continue breathing at this pace.

(30 seconds)

Now let your breath assume its own rhythm that is effortless and relaxing.

(60 seconds)

Your body and mind are becoming more and more relaxed with each breath.

(30 seconds)

Notice your entire body supported by the surface beneath you.

Notice how still your feet are.

Feel them becoming heavy.

(10 seconds)

Imagine your feet getting warm.

Feel the warmth in your feet spreading up your legs.

(5 seconds)

Now, feel your arms becoming heavy and being supported by the surface underneath.

Imagine them sinking in the warmth of your beddings or on your cushions.

Notice as that warmth grows from your hands to the whole arm.

(20 seconds)

Feel the warmth from your legs, and the one from your arms make a connection in your stomach.

Notice your stomach becoming warm.

Notice the warmth spreading to your chest.

Feel the warmth overflowing to your back.

Notice how your back relaxes.

(20 seconds)

Your whole body feels heavy.

Your whole body is warm, and the bed feels cozier.

You feel an urge to cuddle your pillow, but your body is too heavy to move.

(10 seconds)

let your eyes sink heavily behind your eyelids.

They shut allowing you to lock out the external world and to rest.

(10 seconds)

Now, notice the sensations on your forehead.

Your forehead feels cool, calm, and relaxed.

There is no trace of tension on your forehead.

(10 seconds)

Envision tension escaping from your body through your toes and fingers.

Scan for any tension in your head- your eyes, ears, nose, ears, and cheeks.

Notice it flowing out of your body through the fingers.

(10 seconds)

Feel your head relaxing.

(10 seconds)

Become aware of your neck.

Scan for any tension in your neck.

Release it and watch as it flows out of your system through your fingers.

(10 seconds)

Observe your chest.

Can you feel any tension lodged there?

Release it and let it flow out of your body through the fingers.

(10 seconds)

Feel your stomach.

Check for any knots of tension in your stomach.

Visualize the tension going up to your shoulders

Down to your arms

And finally escaping through your fingertips.

(10 seconds)

Become aware of your back.

Check for any tension in the muscles in your back.

Scan for any tension lodged in your spine.

Release all that tension and feel it coming out through your fingers.

(10 seconds)

Listen to your upper body.

Notice how relaxed your upper body is.

(10 seconds)

Become aware of your hips and buttocks.

Check for any tension in your hips and buttocks.

Release the tension in that area.

Visualize as the tension flows down to your legs and comes out through your toes.

(10 seconds)

Feel your thighs.

Notice how strong they feel.

Feel the longest bone in your body- your thigh bone.

Check for any tension in your thigh bone.

Release all the tension in your thighs and feel then relax.

Notice the tension flowing down to your feet and leaving your body through the toes.

Feel your thighs becoming relaxed.

(20 seconds)

Move down further and become aware of your lower legs.

Notice your calves and your shins.

Feel all the muscles and veins in your lower leg.

Feel them tightening under tension.

Release all the tension in your lower legs and feel them becoming heavy.

Watch as the tension is washed out of the legs via the toes.

Feel your lower legs getting relaxed and calm.

(20 seconds)

Divert your attention to your ankles.

Do you feel any tension or pain in your ankles?

Release the tension lodged there and let it flow out through your toes.

(10 seconds)

Move your feet in a circular motion and check for any tension in your feet, soles, and toes.

Notice the areas that are tense and tired.

Release all the tension lodged there and feel your feet relaxing.

Visualize all the tension leaving hurriedly from your body through your toes and fingers.

With every breath you take, you can notice the tension draining away.

With every breath, you can feel the tension exiting through the fingers and toes.

(20 seconds)

Allow your mind to drift and relax.

You don't have to think or concentrate on anything.

Feel your body relaxing more as the tension drains away.

Feel it move through your veins to your fingers and toes.

Empty tension and replace it with relaxation in every part of your body.

(20 seconds)

Notice soft relaxation filling your body and mind.

Notice warm relaxation filling your body and mind.

Your body is becoming dense, and it is sinking deeper.

You are drifting to a pleasant sleep.

(30 seconds)

Gently, breathe in.

And breathe out.

(20 seconds)

Count one to ten

10 seconds

Now, I will begin to count backwards from 100. As I do so, concentrate on the numbers as I count them. (leave 3 seconds between numbers)

100 99 98 97 96 95 94 93 92 91 90 89 88 87 86 85 84 83 82 81 80 79 78 77 76 75 74 73 72 71 70 69 68 67 66 65 64 63 62 61 60 59 58 57 56 54 53 52 51 50 49 48 47 46 45 43 42 41 40 39 38 37…

Maintain your focus on the numbers and keep counting them.

(10 seconds)

Your mind and body are relaxed.

(10seconds)

Maybe you feel sleepy.

(20 seconds)

It is becoming difficult to concentrate on the numbers.

Your mind is wandering.

Your mind wants to rest. Allow it to rest. Drift off to restfulness

(60 seconds)

You are drifting into a pleasant sleep.

With every breath you take, you are more relaxed.

With every breath you take, all you want to do is to sleep.

You are calm and sleepy.

You cannot count any longer.

It is alright; you can drift to sleep.

Surrender to your sleep.

(120 seconds)

Envision a beautiful place that is serene and calm.

Visualize your body floating in this beautiful place that is safe and serene.

(10 seconds)

Notice your body flying through the air gently.

This is the place is restful and peaceful.

(10 seconds)

Slowly rest on the beautiful place and let your body sink in comfortably.

You do not need words to focus anymore.

Simply enjoy the feeling of relaxation.

(90 seconds)

Rest, Rest, Rest.

Chapter 19: Guided Meditation to Instantly Relief Anxiety

Choose a comfortable seating position and sit with your spine straight and feet either on the ground or crossed.

Place your hands on your laps with the palms facing upwards.

(5 seconds)

Gently close your eyes.

(5 seconds)

Become aware of your whole body.

Take note of how your body feels from your head to your toes.

(20 seconds)

Inhale deeply and notice the air going through your nose to your diaphragm.

Hold it for a few seconds and then release the breath.

(5 seconds)

Continue breathing and notice your body relaxing every time you breathe out.

(10 seconds)

Inhale… exhale.

(10 seconds)

Become aware of any thoughts lingering in your mind.

Identify the dominant thoughts in your mind. What is it about?

Thinking is what the mind does. Do not get averse about the thoughts. Just observe them, like a curious onlooker.

(30 seconds)

Take note of the feeling or feelings associated with the dominant thoughts. Identify how those thoughts make you feel.

(30 seconds)

If the thoughts cause you gross sensations or emotions, focus on your breathing. Make your breathing deeper

(30 seconds)

When a positive thought pops in your mind, notice it as well and let it go without clinging to it.

(10 seconds)

You may find your mind wandering to the fears you have about life.

Do not be critical.

Notice it, but do not pursue it.

Notice the thought and let it go.

(30 seconds)

Envision yourself on a beach.

Imagine the sunrays diffusing in your skin.

Notice the breeze blowing your body, making you relax.

(5 seconds)

Visualize your thoughts as the wind.

Continue breathing and notice as the wind blows and stops.

Notice the wind sweeping past you as your thoughts keep changing.

(10 seconds)

Remain calm and keep breathing.

(20 seconds)

Remember that in this life, you are bound to experience anxiety.

You should never fight it.

Instead, welcome the feeling and notice as it is blown away by the wind.

(10 seconds)

When you experience happiness or joy remain aware of the pleasant emotions without clinging to them.

(20 seconds)

Begin to count from 10 to 1.

(20 seconds)

When you feel ready, become aware of the present moment.

Pay attention to your breathing.

(20 seconds)

Wiggle your toes and fingers.

(5 seconds)

Shake your hands and legs.

(5 seconds)

Move your head back and forth and the side to side.

(5 seconds)

Come back to stillness and gently open your eyes.

(5 seconds)

Reacquaint yourself with your immediate environment.

Look around and listen.

When you are ready, get on with the rest of your day.

Chapter 20: Guided Meditation for Calm and Peace

Find a quiet place where you can sit either on the ground with your legs crossed or on a chair with your feet on the ground.

Rest your hands on your lap.

(5 seconds)

Adjust your posture to lengthen your spine and drop your shoulders.

Gently close your eyes.

Take a deep breath in and exhale slowly.

(10 seconds)

Another deep breath in and completely empty your lungs.

(10 seconds)

With each breath let tension melt away from your body.

(20 seconds)

Continue to breathe deeply.

(20 seconds)

Take a deep breath, hold it for a few seconds then release it slowly.

(5 seconds)

Keep breathing deeply in and out.

(20 seconds)

Become aware of the top of your head.

Imagine relaxation flowing from the top of your head and spreading throughout your whole body.

(5 seconds)

Feel your forehead and eyes relaxing.

Notice your jaws releasing tension and softening.

Feel your cheeks becoming warm.

(10 seconds)

Notice as the peaceful sensation flows to your neck.

Feel it massaging your shoulder muscles and releasing tension.

Breathe in.

Breathe out.

(10 seconds)

Feel the peaceful sensation flowing to your arms.

Notice it soothing your arms, hands, and fingers.

(10 seconds)

Become aware of your mind relaxing as your body relaxes.

Notice how your thoughts seem weightless.

(10 seconds)

Observe as the peaceful sensation flows to your chest and belly.

Feel that area getting soothed and relaxed.

As your chest and belly rise with every inhale, it relaxes with every exhale.

(20 seconds)

Feel the peaceful sensation now caressing your back.

Notice all the tension being released from your back.

(10 seconds)

The peaceful sensation keeps flowing.

It is now relaxing your buttocks.

(10 seconds)

Visualize it flowing to your thighs.

It slides slowly to the back of your thighs.

It slides gently to the front of your thighs.

It relaxes your thighs completely.

(10 seconds)

The soothing sensation flows to your knees.

Feel it relaxing your knees.

Feel it softening the knee cap.

(10 seconds)

It picks its momentum and flows to your calves. Washing away any tension in your calves.

(5 seconds)

It slides into your shin.

It relieves all the tension lodged in your shin.

(10 seconds)

Become aware of your ankles.

Check for any strain or pain in your ankles.

Notice the peaceful sensation relaxing your ankles.

(10 seconds)

It now flows to your feet.

Notice it relaxing your feet.

(10 seconds)

Notice how your body feels calm and peaceful.

(30 seconds)

Envision yourself on a beach.

Notice the sun warming your face and body.

Feel the sand beneath your feet.

(5 seconds)

You are all alone on this beach.

It is serene

Listen to the sound of the ocean.

(10 seconds)

You notice a small boat on the shore and walk towards it.

Get into the boat and let the waves rock the boat into the waters.

You take a boat ride towards the island on the Far East.

Enjoying the sunshine and the breeze from the ocean.

(5 seconds)

You arrive at your destination and step out of the boat.

The sublime beauty of the island takes your breath

(5 seconds)

The view of the exotic birds and colored flowers.

(5 seconds)

The palm trees surrounding the island provide a scenic view.

(5 seconds)

In this place, you feel free and peaceful.

(10 seconds)

You notice a path leading into the heart of the island.

You follow it as you continue to soak up the beauty of the island.

(10 seconds)

At the center of the island, you notice a pool. You move towards it and undress before stepping into the waters.

(5 seconds)

With each step you take in to the pool, you feel more peaceful and calm.

(10 seconds)

You glide in the water and feel your thoughts melting away.

(10 seconds)

You are now peaceful and relaxed. You allow yourself to rest here and savor the beauty and serenity of this place.

(60seconds)

When you are ready to leave, you walk back to the boat, and ride back to the mainland bring along the peace and calm you experienced in the island.

(60seconds)

Slowly, become aware of your present moment.

Listen to your heartbeat.

Notice the warmth in your hands.

Wiggle your toes and fingers.

Gently open your eyes.

Conclusion

Life is beautiful but also there are times when it is challenging and overwhelming.

The memories of the past can bring us much joy and nostalgia, yet they can be the one thing that holds us back from living fully now.

Likewise, the future can be a hopeful place we anxiously or excitedly look forward to, but today and now is all we are assured of.

Meditation reminds us to enjoy the now and make the most of it just as it is.

It may not make every moment perfect or take away all your problems, but it gives you a tool to enable you make the most of now. It can make each day a little better and at times "a little" better is enough.

It is a skill and the more you practice the better you become at it.

While there is scientific evidence to show that indeed meditation is a great tool for improving your quality of life, all the research and studies do not matter if meditation remains a concept in your life. Give it a fair chance in your life. Be patient with the process. Remain consistent. Find a way to fit it in the most natural way to your lifestill.it will pay off.

I hope that this practice brings you a little bit calm, joy, centeredness, courage, hope, clarity and any other good in your life.

May you be happy,

May you be peaceful,

May you be harmonious.